WWJD NOW?

What Would Jesus Do Now?

Garrett Ward Sheldon

WWJD-NOW?

By

Garrett W. Sheldon

With

Greg Sergent & James Cox

Copyright 2024
ISBN: 978-0-9966890-9-0

Softcover

No part of this book may be reproduced or transmitted in any form or by any means, electronic or mechanical, including photocopying, recording, or by any information storage and retrieval system without permission in writing from the copyright owner.

All scripture verses are from the:
King James Version (KJV)
New King James Version (NKJV)
New American Standard Version (NASV)
New Living Translation (NLT)
The Amplified Bible (AMP)

Hopeway Publishers

Preface

In 1896, my great grandfather, Charles M. Sheldon, wrote the book *IN HIS STEPS*, which challenged Christians to ask "What Would Jesus Do?" whenever facing a problem or decision. He felt this personal discipleship idea was inspired of God. That book soon sold an estimated 30 million copies in 20 languages, making it the best-selling Christian book after the Bible. Because of a faulty copyright, he made no money from this book but rejoiced that the WWJD message touched so many hearts around the world.

About a hundred years later, I felt led to update *IN HIS STEPS* as *"What Would Jesus Do?* which became part of a great WWJD movement in the 1990s. Recently, I felt led to update my novel 30 years after the original as *What Would Jesus Do NOW?* The world has changed so much in the past 30 years that Christians face a whole new set of challenges (addiction of all kinds; mental health problems; relationship and moral issues; stress and depression). Though our online, remote age raises new problems, Jesus still provides the answers: truth; healing; peace; comfort, and love. This update of this classic story gives a few examples of people finding answers to life, and joy, through asking that simple question: "What would Jesus do in my place?" I pray it will encourage you to lead this immediate life of Faith, seek God's will for your life through the Bible, the Holy Spirit, and the church, and see the many blessings and happiness of this Godly life!

Garrett W. Sheldon

Chapter One

The Loss

Tim Chapman unlocked the church door and walked back to his office, humming a happy tune. It was Monday morning, and he was thinking of the glorious church service Sunday morning: the magnificent music on the Steinway piano, sunlight streaming through the stained-glass windows, praise songs with gorgeous videos on the screens, prayers, and fellowship.

But the most significant event was a visitor: a young man, a drug addict in his 20s but looking like a 90-year-old corpse—thin, sickly, like so many "meth-heads" that wandered the streets of this small city. Ted Hicks was his name.

Though attendance has been down about half since the COVID-19 epidemic, the church welcomed him and provided him with prayer, money, food, and a night at the local Country Joy motel. Today, Rev. Tim thought, they would find him permanent housing, a job, and new clothes.

Then the office phone rang. Tim picked it up.

"Pastor, this is Bill at the motel! Don't ever send any more of your druggies here! He invited four of his buddies to his room at 2:00 am to party—tore the place up. We had to call the police. They're all in prison now! The cops found drugs, guns, stolen goods, and prostitutes in the room. Don't EVER send anyone to the motel again, REVEREND!"

Tim put down the phone and wandered, dazed, down the hall into the church sanctuary.

Chapter Two

The Song

Behind the pulpit was a young, beautiful woman: Loni Lamm, a gifted singer, songwriter, and actress, practicing her Special song for next Sunday. Loni saw the preacher walk into the back of the church, his head down.

"What is the matter, Pastor Tim? You look upset and depressed!"

The minister struggled with words,

"Loni, I can't believe it. That drug addict we had here yesterday is back in prison after we thought we'd helped him. I just don't know what to do. What would God have us do with these problems? We've tried everything we know to do. Nothing's worked! What would Jesus do? What would Jesus Christ have us do? Help us, Lord!"

Loni's clear, beautiful voice began to sing, composing as she sang:

> "Oh Lord, please tell me
> What would Jesus do?
> With the addicted, the lonely and depressed
> To the lost and the hurt
> Would He bend low to touch their heart?
> Teach their soul which way to go.

Lord, please guide me and show me the way
To go about my everyday
Showing Your love and sharing Your name
Oh Lord, tell me, what would Jesus do.

Oh Lord, please tell me
How I can make a difference
To help those you love and show them Your love
My Lord, show me by Your Word and Spirit
To do what Jesus would do.

Give me the wisdom of Solomon
Give me the boldness of Esther
Guide me on the righteous path
Lord, give me the compassion as
Jesus gave to the woman at the well.
O Lord, tell me what Jesus would do ?"*

The strong, clear, tender voice awakened Pastor Tim.

"Loni! Sing that song for your Special on Sunday! I'm going to preach on that! It's perfect! It's an answer to prayer!"

*Composed by Madison Denhardt & Lonijonli Fox HONEYSUCKLE DREAM.

Chapter Three

The Question

Loni's stirring, passionate voice left most of the congregation in tears the following Sunday. Rev. Tim preached on the theme, "What Would Jesus Do?" He began with the Bible Scripture John 10:27.

"Jesus said, 'Follow me.' As Christians, we are to take on any situation in our lives, any problem, tragedy, or suffering, and follow Him.

After a great defeat here last week, God showed us that one way to follow Jesus is for us and the church to ask ourselves, 'What would Jesus Do in my place?' What would Jesus have me to do, with family, friends, co-workers, and strangers? In every decision, we ask, 'What would Jesus do?' His love, forgiveness, truth with our problems, fears, failures, confusion, depression, stress, addiction?

He said, 'Ask and it shall be given.' We believe, and the Bible teaches, that the moment of faith in Jesus as the Son of God, God as man, but a man without sin. So He can take our sin and its punishment, death, and hell upon Himself on the Cross. So we have forgiveness of our sins and can spend eternity in heaven with a Holy God and have His Holy Spirit within us here– NOW as Guide, Comforter, Teacher. So, the Spirit of Jesus within us can give us the answers to what we should do to

please God, serve Him, fulfill the plan He has for our lives, and have true happiness.
So, I challenge each of you with that question whenever you face a decision or problem: What would Jesus Do? Then, receive the answers from God: guidance, strength, patience, and joy. Amen!"

Chapter Four

The Meeting

After the closing hymn, most church members talked about the WWJD challenge. Pastor Tim then went to his study for the monthly deacon board meeting with twelve parish lay leaders. This clergy study was a warm, comfortable, homey room with a sofa and large chairs, bookcases with many volumes of theology, history, and the Bible, paintings and crosses on the walls, and trinkets on the shelves from Jerusalem, Ireland, and England. Large windows looking out on beautiful trees!

The head deacon, Russ Turnbull, a large, rough man, and wealthy local businessman, opened the meeting: "Pastor Tim, this WWJD stuff is ridiculous and stupid. It can't be done! It's presumptuous to think we can know what Jesus would do."

"Well, Russ," Tim replied "our faith teaches that when we come to Christ, His Spirit comes within us and is a teacher, guide, and Comforter. And we have His teaching in the Bible, especially the Sermon on the Mount (Matthew 5-6), and fellow Christians, present and past to advise us. All that says we can know what Jesus would have us do. Doing it may be harder–with our sin and selfishness, but His Holy Spirit can help us there, too, if we ask."

"I don't know," Russ said glaringly. He was a prominent powerful man, the owner of Turnbull Industries, wealthy and influential. "We need to consider increasing our numbers, which are down by half, and our finances."

"To do that", Jeb String, a Data Analyst from a local survey marketing firm, added, "we need to know our clientele group, its trends, and demographics. I'm not sure this WWJD thing will have 'attract-ability.'"

Joe McClue, a retired banker, said, "I think the Pastor's message is inspired—listen to the congregation's excitement! It makes our faith personal and relevant. I accept that challenge!"

Helen Hicks, an Administrator from the nearby college, said, "RELEVANT"! "Where's our defense of transgender rights?"!

"But sister," Tim replied, "the Bible says God made us male and female (Genesis 2)".

"And what about Islamophobia? What are we doing about that?! Helen continued.

"But Helen," Tim replied "God said to Abram and his people Israel. "I will bless those who bless you and curse those who curse you (Genesis 12.3).

"And what about Equity?" Helen shouted.

"What's that?" Russ asked. "I've heard that term in business and politics, but I don't know what it means." She interjected, "It means all are equal, can be anything, do anything, regardless of background or training. Any preference is discrimination!"

"Well, Helen, the Bible says we are all equal as members of Christ, but we have different gifts and abilities and need each other," Tim explained.

"Yes," Molly Jennedy, a practical nurse at the nearby hospital, said, "Paul compares the church to a body– the different parts need each other and honor each other. She opened her Bible, flipped through, and said, "Here it is in 1 Corinthians 12 'the eye cannot say to the hand, I have no need of you,' and the manifestation of the Spirit is given to for the profit of all...wisdom, knowledge, faith, healing...but one and the same Spirit works all those things.' So we have many different gifts and talents, but are one in Christ!"

"Well, that's just discrimination and 'privilege'!" Helen shouted and stormed out of the office, slamming the door.

"Is there anything else before we close in prayer?" Pastor Tim asked.

Chapter Five

Sunday Dinner

Tim arrived home at about 2:30. Nancy, his wife, greeted him. "Hi, honey; did the meeting run late?"

"Yes," he replied. "Were they as excited as everyone else about that WWJD challenge?"

"Well, some were, and some weren't," Tim replied.

"Well, dinner is ready–chicken and dumplings, sweet peas, mashed potatoes, salad, and your favorite: homemade chocolate pudding!"

"Yum," said Tim, smelling the rich aroma of delicious food. "I am SO exhausted and starving after Sunday service! Where's Eric?"

"As usual, he's in his room, on those video games on his phone, It's like he's ADDICTED!"

"Addicted?" Tim replied, reminds me of a story Professor Don told me last week.

One of his best students, a brilliant girl from West Africa, suddenly stopped coming to class and is flunking out! He saw her in the hall and asked what was going on. "I'm sorry, Professor, I'm on this video game until 4 am and then sleep through class! I think it's called 'Sandy-Smash.' I like sand and I like smashing things!"

"Shelly told me other teachers have lost their jobs because they're hooked on computer games, sites, and social media and forget to show up for work."

"Why don't you ask some other moms if you could have kids' activities: sports, games, picnics together, personal real relationships?" Tim suggested.

"Eric, dinner honey," his mom shouted. The six-year-old boy came into the dining room looking at his phone.

"Now put that down, son, and have dinner."

After saying the blessing, Nancy served Sunday dinner, which was enjoyed by all. After dinner, Eric picked up his phone and headed back to his room. His father said, "Hey, buddy, let's go out in the yard and throw a ball around."

Chapter Six

What Would Jesus Do NOW?

During the following week, Pastor Tim heard many stories of the effect of that question, led by the Spirit of Christ. Nancy did talk to the moms of some of Eric's friends, and soon they were having kids' gatherings for sports, games, meals, and parties. Personal. Real. Supervised. Encouraging Christian community and values.

On Monday morning, Tim got a call from Ralph Rosano, a church member in his 50's and a prominent local CPA. "Rev. Tim, I wanted to tell you that I've been offered a big job in California (2000 miles away) with double my salary!"

Well, Ralph, we'll miss you at the church."

"But I turned the job down. My children and grandchildren live here, and it's more important to be near family than more money."

"That's great, Ralph!" Tim exclaimed, "God emphasizes the importance of family throughout the Bible."

"And it's because I asked, 'What would Jesus do' in my place? It seems He said something about 'the love of money is the root of all evil!'"

"Indeed, Ralph, the world and the devil tempt us with money, power, and prestige, but we end up less happy than with more valuable things, family, friends, purpose, and peace of mind. You've made a good decision, and you won't regret it."

It was about noon, so Tim got up from his desk and headed out to lunch. Suddenly someone raced into the office and slammed the door behind him. It was Nick Feeler, a church member in his 30's. He looked wild and disheveled: messy, dirty clothes and hair, a strong odor, unshaven.

"Pastor, I need to talk to you!" This man had grown up in this church, whose parents and grandparents had been prominent members.

"Sure, Nick, have a seat. What's up?"

"Everything I say is between us, ok?!, like with a lawyer or counselor. Good," he breathed heavily, "I'm in trouble. Ever since you preached on following Jesus, I can't sleep, think."

"What's the problem, Nick?" Pastor Tim said gently.

"I'm in a mess, drinking all the time, having affairs with three women at work and two in the neighborhood, and, ah, oh," Nick broke down crying, "I've been stealing money at work!"

"I just can't resist the 'high' of booze or the temptation of sex—-it's everywhere —where we used to say 'hi' or shake hands, everyone has quick sex! Everywhere. The excitement, but then the guilt, fear, craziness."

"Well, Nick, God's plan is for us to have sex in a committed relationship–marriage, and to be faithful. There are emotional and spiritual dimensions to intimacy–you can't separate them from the physical lust. It will drive you crazy: The devil tempts you with an ounce of pleasure and you end up with a ton of pain. Now, what about this stealing money?"

Nick, again breaking down in tears, said, "It started with a little from the cash drawer, then fixing the books."

"How much?"

"Oh, just a couple thousand…"

"Well, Nick, you know you'll get caught, and then what ruin? Prison?"

"I don't get it, just weak, I guess, What do I do, reverend?"

"Well, you've done the most important thing, Nick: confession and repentance. God says, in First John, 'If we confess our sins, He is faithful and just to forgive us our sins and cleanse us from all unrighteousness.' We all have to confess our sins, even evil thoughts, to God daily and ask Him to strengthen us to resist those sins and lead a moral life which is the only true happiness."

Tim added, "Otherwise, I recommend avoiding areas of temptation. Go home and throw out the liquor bottles, stay away from bars and liquor stores. And girls…
I'd think about getting married, Nick. A good wife will protect you from the other women!"

"As for the money, stop stealing and figure out how you can restore it."

"Thank you, Pastor," Nick cried.

"Let's have a prayer," Tim said. He got the small bottle of anointing oil from Jerusalem, scented with frankincense. He put a drop on his finger and applied it to Nick's forehead, making the sign of the cross.

"In the name of the Father, the Son and the Holy Spirit. Lord, look with mercy on your servant, your child, forgive him of his sins by the grace of Jesus, STRENGTHEN him to resist further temptations and sins. Show him how to make restitution. When he slips, may he quickly repent and return to you by the power of your Holy Spirit. Amen"

They hugged, and Nick left with a peace he hadn't felt in years. Hopeful. Happy.

Over the next few months. Nick, despite some slips, grew in faith and holiness. He worshipped, prayed regularly, read his Bible, and even began to lead worship, give messages, and fill in sermons when Pastor Tim was away.

At lunch, Tim ran into Emma Byrd, a retired school teacher. "Pastor, I can't get that WWJD message out of my mind–to live our Christian lives purposefully, directly, to show Christ's love to all around us. I'm trying to show them love displayed in First Corinthians 13—to be patient, kind, not proud or envious, to rejoice in the good, not the bad. I even forgave those who hate me not returning evil for evil. I have a new attitude toward my family, friends, and even strangers."

"That's great Emma!"

She leaned over and whispered in his ear "I just left that waitress at $20 tip–for a $20 lunch! I remember how hard it was working as a server–I was a waitress in college, and how mean people could be."

Look at her—she's in shock, Emma; "Bless you."

The next day, Jake Mulligan texted him a long message at 4 in the morning. A bright, successful lawyer in his late 20's, Jake rambled on about being hooked to online games, chats, porn, sport and gambling. It was tearing up his law practice, marriage, and mental health. What should he do? What would Jesus do?

Pastor Tim texted back, "Thanks, Jake, come by my church study to talk and pray." He never showed up. A month later, he was found dead-suicide. On Friday morning, Rev. Tim walked into his church sanctuary to find Loni moaning a song.

"What's up Loni?"

"Pastor, Tim, I've just made the hardest decision of my life! Do you know that Christian movie I made last year? Well, a producer from Hollywood called and offered me the lead in another movie–with big names, lots of money, and future fame! All I've dreamed of. Then I looked at the script, and it was full of nudity, profanity, immorality, and darkness. It was such a temptation: Imagine fame, wealth, power, attention. But I prayed and realized God didn't want me to prostitute the gifts of singing and acting to evil. But I'm sad and disappointed. Will I just be a minor singer, actress in a church, and low-budget films?"

"Sister", Tim said, "You made the right decision and won't regret it. God will honor you and bless you in ways you can't imagine."

"Thanks, Pastor", she sobbed, "that helps."

Chapter Seven

Misery

Tim went to his monthly doctor's appointment with talented D.O. Dan Joshland that Friday afternoon. This "chiropractor" M.D. kept Tim's back aligned and out of pain after a bad injury 30 years before lifting heavy carpet while moving house. Dr. Dan "aligned" his spine, relieving pain and tension without drugs. Tim had also learned to stretch, use Chinese acupressure points, and controlled breathing techniques for stress and sleep.

Before seeing the doctor, he was in the examining room while the nurse, a woman in her mid-40s, checked his weight and blood pressure. Usually cheerful, she suddenly broke down crying. Tim noticed his blood pressure going way up. "Is there anything wrong?" he asked her.

"Just my husband meeting a woman online–2000 miles away—and now he's moved there. They're having an affair, and he wants a divorce," she sobbed. "Well," she shouted in anger; "I'm going to give him a divorce! I talked to the toughest lawyer in town; he said I can get EVERYTHING: the house, kids, money, his business. Get this, the lawyer checked his business and found some irregularities so–he could go to jail! He'll wake up in prison–lost his home, family, money, business, and, I'm sure by then, his girlfriend! How will he feel then?"

"I know you hurt," Tim said, "but do you really want vengeance? If you show him love and forgiveness you might find he returns. I've seen it many times." "Vengeance is MINE, saith the Lord." (Romans 12:19).

"I don't know...I just don't know," she wept. "Oh, the doctor will see you now."

Tim went home exhausted, arriving at 4 o'clock to find young Eric with his Aunt Minnie. "Nancy's at the Hairdresser; she should have been home by now."

"Don't worry: I'm home now. Go on home, and I'll watch the boy." Eric returned to his cell phone games.

"Hey buddy," his father said, "put that down, and let's watch some T.V., get a snack, and I'll put in an Andy Griffith Show DVD."

"Oh, boy," something with Barney—he's funny!" They watched and laughed together.

At 6 p.m., Tim's wife and mother showed up. "I'm so sorry I'm late, honey. The beauty parlor was packed with old women getting their hair and makeup done. My three o'clock trim didn't start until 5:00!"

"What were they all doing there on a Friday afternoon? Tim asked. Were they going to a party or reunion?"

"I don't know," Nancy sighed. "They were all shouting and laughing so loud I couldn't make it out. It sounded something like 'Fruity Date.'"

"Maybe they are all going to the Farmer's Market; no, that's Thursday afternoon in town. "

Chapter 8

The Temple

The Women's Study Group met at the church every Wednesday evening, led by one of the twenty in attendance. This month, Molly Jennedy, the County Nurse, led a study on the TEMPLE OF GOD.

She began, "it says in First Corinthians 3:16, that our bodies are the Temple of God! What does that mean?"

Rhonda Arendt looked at the Scripture and said, "Because the Spirit of God dwells within us. Oh, I see like the Temple in Jerusalem, God is in there. Like. . . a great cathedral, Notre Dame has beautiful Gothic arches, stained glass windows, candles, and music. The Holy Lord dwells in there. Or an Early American Church: red brick with white columns, large windows, and white pews: the House of God. So how do we take care of those sacred places?"

"We maintain them, clean them," Sally Birch, a secretary, chimed in. "We don't let them get run down, dirty, or neglected."

"So how shall we care for our bodies–The Temples of God?" Molly led the discussion.

"I guess keep them healthy, clean, and neat."

"Right," the nurse said," and every day, I see the neglect of our bodies: unhealthy foods, poor lifestyle, lack of exercise, and bad habits that weaken and destroy these body temples. Half the American population has been obese all ages—mostly from processed food—carbohydrates with God-given fiber removed, sweeteners, and chemicals that mess up our whole system. What the Old Testament called adulterated food—ruined! All of this fuels obesity, diabetes, cancer..."

Sally Fields, a high school sophomore, chimed in: "And stress: people say the meanest things online, gossip, vicious, hatred about others! The things you would never say to someone in person! It really hurts to hear what others are saying against you. I cry, I'm hurt. It's like being killed. Didn't Jesus say if we had hatred toward others, we have committed murder? This 'venting' of feeling online is murder!"

"And don't forget mental illness," Brandy Rigges, a 20-year-old college student, said. "All my friends are suffering from anxiety, depression, sleeplessness. We are bombarded with a million demands and expectations: we're supposed to be successful executives and professionals, sexy, wives and mothers, everything! What's our identity?"

Most of my friends work five jobs: 2 onsite and 3 online."

"Yes," Molly added, "I see it every day at the hospital: addiction, suicide attempts. Then, What are we supposed to do?"

"As Christians, we are to seek God's plan and way for our lives. I think He gives us each talents and gifts, and developing and using those gives us meaning, peace, and happiness in our lives. The Bible says we should have committed, long-term relationships, loving marriages, and families. Jesus said 'Come unto me all who are burdened and I will give you rest' (Matthew 11: 28). Let's see how He gives us rest and peace."

She opened her Bible to Proverbs 31:10-31–this describes a Godly woman: faithful to her husband, a loving mother, providing a prosperous household: involved in commerce, diligent, kind, wise, adorned by her husband and children.

"Yeah" screamed Brandy, "well that requires a good man. Where are they? All my boyfriends cheated on me, lied, and hurt me!"

"Well, they're all online chatting with dozens of girls! So, the girls are getting online to sell their bodies! I heard the average webcam girl makes $40 an hour—that's more than working in a restaurant or a store!" Emma muttered.

"But how does that make them feel?" Molly asked, "Like sluts – Unrespected, used, miserable."

"Right; so, it's better to lead a Godly life and wait for a good man."

"Well, that's a long wait!" Brandy cried. "How did you do it, Gwendolyn?", Speaking to one of the few women in the room with a nice husband.

Gwendolyn replied, "I don't know; I had plenty of disappointments before meeting Bill. Ultimately, I think it's God's grace, trying to keep Godly standards and keep looking. I heard even Christian dating sites can be frauds—full of predators!"

Molly concurred. "I think prayer, Godly living, a church community, and hope."

"In the long run," Hannah added, "faithful, committed relationships are happier, but it's hard in this crazy wicked world. But God promises us peace and comfort through His Holy Spirit, if we are patient and wait upon Him. 'Peace I leave with you; my peace I give unto you, not as the world gives' (John 14:27)."

Chapter 9

Blackmail

Russ Turnbull opened the front door of his suburban mansion and let his sister Phyllis in. She was a middle-aged mother of five and carried a casserole dish with her. "Here's a dinner for you!"

Since Russ's wife Hilda had died 2 years before, of cancer, Phyllis had regularly brought her brother's meals. She looked around his enormous living room and kitchen a mess of papers, bottles trash. "Russ, you have to clean this place!"

"The housekeeper Mildred is coming in tomorrow; she'll do it."

"Why don't you let me fix you up with one of my friends– most of them would make wonderful wives."

"I don't want a wife!" Russ shouted. "The last one just complained, bossed me around, and made my life miserable. I thought the Bible said wives should respect and submit to their husbands!"

"It also said husbands should love their wives as Christ loved the church and gave Himself for it. It's mutual."

"Well, I don't need a wife; I've got a housekeeper and plenty of girlfriends!"

"GIRLFRIENDS?!" Phylis looked aghast at her elderly, heavy, rather ugly brother. "I never see you with girlfriends!"

"They're all online, cute, available all the time for whatever I want—Sixty of them!"

"Sixty? What do you do with all these distant women?"

"Oh," Russ smiled. "Chat and look at each other..."

"Impersonal, remote, temporary, you call those relationships? Our faith and heritage say we need permanent, personal, committed, loving marriages. That's where true happiness and security come from."

"I'll take the web girls, thanks."

"And another thing," brother, "I've heard your private online affairs can become public to your embarrassment, shame, and even social, financial ruin!"

"Li Ching wouldn't do that; she's really cute! And nice!"

"I'm warning you," Phyllis said and left.

Russ went to his computer and pulled up some of his "friends". A strange message came from one of the sites showing various photos of himself and Li Ching.
"Transfer half a million dollars to this account within 24 hours or these pictures will be made public."

Russ stared in shock, his eyes bulging and his heart pounding. He didn't know what to do, but quickly deleted all his other girlfriends.

Chapter 10

Youth Revival

It was Saturday morning 8 o'clock and Pastor Tim was at home in his study, as usual, writing his Sunday sermon. A cup of tea beside him, soft Christian music playing, two candles burning on the hearth, reminding him of the church he grew up in. An atmosphere of peace, calm, quiet and contemplation always settled his soul after a busy week.

As always, he found that with the chosen Bible verse and the flow of the Holy Spirit, the words came quickly written with his fountain pen on white sheets of paper. Just as he was finishing, a knock came at the door. "Yes", he called out.

"Pastor, it's me Kevin Hall, can I talk with you?"

"Sure, come on in." Kevin was a Junior at Central School and member of the church, excitedly walked in.

"What can I do for you?"

"Well, Pastor, a group of my friends were wondering if we could have a youth service at the church Sunday evenings. Many of feel like getting together for worship, praise, prayers and testimonies."

"Sure", Tim said.

"And if you open with a brief message, we'd appreciate it."

"Sure, love to."

"OK!" Kevin shouted, "See you at 7!"

That evening, Tim was surprised to see "a few friends" filled up the 300-seat sanctuary. Mostly high school students—talking, laughing and walking around.

The service started with a rousing praise band, everyone singing, clapping and cheering.

Kevin introduced the minister.

"Welcome to First Church", Tim said, from behind the pulpit. "It's great to see all of you here!"

After a brief prayer, he opened with one of his favorite verses, John 10:10. "Jesus says, 'The Thief comes to steal, kill and destroy, but I have come that you may have life and life more abundantly,' repeating, 'I have come that you may have life, and life more abundant.'"

Tim continued "The thief is the Devil, the world and our sin. It kills physically, mentally, and spiritually, but Jesus has come to give us LIFE–physical health, healing, mental peace, joy, clarity; and above all spiritual life: insight, guidance, comfort, and community. Jesus, God, overcomes the Devil!"

"The world's temptations and lies, and our sin's evil and pain. He restores our souls, and creates, loving, committed relationships, a sense of purpose, and amazing joy!"

"I often say, that the Devil lies about sin, that it will give us pleasure, power, wealth, fame, prestige, actually sin is an ounce of pleasure and a ton of pain. He, and the world's deceits and our own weaknesses and sin tempt us to break God's moral law, to take what we desire, steal, cheat, but misery, guilt, addiction, and death follow.

Jesus forgives us our sin, takes its penalty, death and hell on the cross, so we can have forgiveness of our sin and start a new life of holiness and true happiness. He gives His Holy Spirit, within believer as a guide, helper, teacher, comforter in this hard, cruel and confused world. 'Cast all your cares on Him; for He cares for you' (1Peter: 5,7)."

"It isn't always easy, we have needs; we are tempted, deceived, but God says in 1 John 1:9, 'If we confess our sin, He is faithful and just to forgive us our sins and to cleanse us of all unrighteousness.' When you slip, repent, confess your sin unto Almighty God. He will forgive you again and cleanse you from all unrighteousness. He will strengthen you morally, physically, emotionally, spiritually, to grow in the faith and godly living and achieve real happiness. Amen!"

A cheer arose in the church, joy, crying, laughing, hugging, waving hands. Kevin got up on the stage and said, tears in his eyes, "Thank you, Pastor!" He asked if anyone wanted to share a testimony, pray, sing or share a word.

Then hundreds of teens came forward to the altar, some falling on their knees, weeping and praying. Others gathered in groups of five and singing, crying, worshiping, praying for one another. Overheard were cries of pain from past sin, abuse, anxiety, and depression.

The Spirit ministered to these with peace, joy and even laughter. Hugs and smiles were exchanged. One by one, young people came up to the stage took the mic and spoke.

One young man, perhaps 16 years old said, with sobs, "my parents divorced last year– I'm torn up by it. I know they had their problems, but we're a FAMILY—my identity and security are with them being together."

A young woman about 14 cried "I was sexually abused by my step-Father. I'm mixed up and hurt, angry and sad. I cannot relate to boys now; afraid I hurt myself, drink, and can't sleep."

Another girl cried "I got an abortion—killed my own baby! Don't believe the lie that this is not a person; I see now, I have nightmares, hate myself!"

"You can have forgiveness through Jesus Christ" Kevin said.

Others confessed sins of stealing, lying, assault. In the background Loni sang softly of God's love and mercy, forgiveness and new life in Christ.

Pastor Tim came up to the mic afterwards and said, "the tragedy, hurt of human life we all have, but as I quoted Jesus, "The thief, Devil came to kill, steal and destroy, but I have come to give you life and life more abundant! Christ can heal; and calm. God's love is a new beginning, joy, and purpose. The importance of Godly love, marriage, and family expressed in the Bible is revealed here–the cost of following the world's ways of temporary pleasure, and selfishness, when true happiness lies in God's truth and law and way".

The room lit up with joy and everyone freely worshiped along with the praise band—clapping, shouting, and praising God.

These nightly youth meetings occurred almost every night for four months, until summer with plans to resume with school in the fall.

At the last revival, a visitor walked up to the stage. Rev. Tim vaguely recognized him, tall, thin, young, but now happy healthy looking.

"Reverend Tim? Remember Me? I am Ted Hicks, the drug addict, you helped me and I ended up back in jail. I'm out now and saved. A fellow meth-head attended one of these services and witnessed to me of God's love, forgiveness, and healing. I'm free in Jesus! I'm no longer in bondage to drugs, enslaved by a substance and system. Thank you, Pastor!"

"Thank you, brother, and thank you God for saving this sinner. Now he can witness to others in bondage to addiction and death!" All cheered at this victory, and another one followed.

Russ Turnbull, the old rich, mean man, walked up to the stage and took the mic from Pastor Tim. With choking words, he said, "I thought of myself as a Good Christian—I attended church, tithed, held all the right views. When Tim preached on WWJD–asking ourselves 'What Would Jesus Do?' When we made any decision, I ridiculed it."

"Seeing this move of the Holy Spirit, I see I've been a fake Christian–I haven't showed the love of Christ in my most immediate relationships: family, employees, strangers. I only hope" he broke down in tears and gasps. "I only hope I live long enough to show others the love of Christ as I did hatred, indifference, envy and pride.

And after the testimony of the young men freed from drug addiction, I'm going to put my wealth behind it! I just read of a Christian drug recovery center in Philadelphia, where addicts can get cleaned up, physically, mentally, and most of all, spiritually–grow in the knowledge of the love of Christ.

I own the old abandoned orphanage on the hill outside Stuffield—you've seen it—looks like a monastery up there. I'm going to restore it–bring in some staff from that Philadelphia Center and some of these local boys cured of addiction and we are going to by the power of God provide healing and renewal."

Cheers and tears closed this revival with Loni singing again *What Would Jesus Do?*

Chapter 11

Recovery

Four months later, the Christian Recovery House opened and Rev Tim and Russ visited it. Already it had a staff of four—Director, Manager, and Counselors: all recovered drug addicts by the grace and healing and power of Christ!

The old three-story building on a hill had been refurbished, repaired and painted. Local churches and donors gave generously.

Tim walked through the vast long hallways, rooms, closets, a big kitchen and dining hall, chapel, comfortable living room and twelve bedrooms upstairs. Already ten inmates were there—hearing about it in jail or on the street. Interviewed by the staff, ready to commit to drug-free Christian rehab: 6-12 months terms, daily routines of prayer meals, work, service, worship, counseling sessions—A physical moral and spiritual healing.

Tim sat down with the members in a comfortable living room, couches, tables and chairs, window looking out on the spacious green ground, quiet and beautiful.

"I'm just curious, me, how you got addicted to drugs and how Jesus freed you?" Tim asked.

Every resident told his story. Tim's eyes teared as he heard the tales of a crisis here, trouble there, then gradual relief from alcohol, then mild drugs, then hard drug addiction, unable to get off, enslaved to a substance! Then broken relationships, marriages, families, kids: crime, jail, sickness. What surprised Tim the most was these men mostly in their 20's were so "normal"--average; not slum, gang members, impoverished, uneducated victims. They were average men. Some had some physical or emotional pain— usually childhood abuse or parents divorcing, but most had normal lives before getting into drugs for fun, pleasure, to be cool.

And the stories of deliverance: a miraculous vision of Christ beckoning and soothing; a sudden visit of a friend or stranger to help, pray.

Tim left exhausted and a bit in shock, but revived and joyful at the Lord's work. One of the great problems of our time —drug addiction was being healed by God and His Spirit working through His servants.

Chapter 12

Attack

When school resumed in the fall, youth revival began again at the church almost every night, hundreds of high school and college students praising God, praying, weeping, confessing, and testifying to freedom and healing through Jesus. News of the Drug Recovery House spread across the region and other such facilities were started, like the youth revival, across the nation.

Then, suddenly the attack began. YouTube videos, online sites and chats, print media, and television began denouncing this move of God's Spirit as fraud, hype, cults, fake, lies, and deception.

A group of local media, TV, blogs, newspapers asked to interview Pastor Tim.

"Aren't you making this all up to get money Reverend?!" One reporter shouted.

Tim, shocked, said, "Ah, no. Actually, the extra services, meals, and outreach are costing the church money. But it's worth it."

Another media leader yelled "Do you think you're God? Are you enjoying all this publicity and fame?"

"Heh," another asked "Isn't this just a cult and you're the cult leader?"

"No" Tim replied, "this is God's Spirit and we give all the Glory to Him!"

"Sure" another angry voice asserted "Isn't it funded, like that so-called Christian Drug Rehab, by right-wing groups, fascists, and Bible fanatics?"

"I really don't think so" Tim muttered, "our donations mostly come from churches and individuals."

"Aren't you teaching hatred of non-Christian lifestyles and groups?" A woman blogger screamed.

"We teach God's grace, love and healing through Christ," Tim replied.

"That's hate speech, intolerance!" She screamed.
An hour later Tim left the news conference with a headache and heartache.

What would Jesus Do, Now, he thought: Celebration on the one side: ridicule on the other. He opened the Bible and read the passages on Jesus' miracle of multiplying the loaves and the fishes (Mark 6). After this and other of Christ wonders, He received crowds of praise and then attacks of ridicule. Often, as after His baptism and before temptation by the Devil and other times, Jesus went up alone to the mountain, the wilderness to pray to God and meditate.

Paster Tim felt "I should follow Jesus' example and during intense times of ministry, retreat to the mountains, the woods alone, to be alone with God pray, rest." There now were many who could fill the pulpit, preach, teach, and visit, (Russ, Molly, Kevin, Ted) for a few weeks while he went away on a spiritual retreat—to his family summer cabin in the woods of northern Wisconsin!

Chapter 13

Retreat

As Tim's car climbed up the hilly four-lane, country highway north, he soon began to feel the stress of the past months lift, calm joy filling his mind as he listened to his favorite sacred music: Haydn's St Nicholas Mass—heavenly music and message!

For two days he navigated small country roads, passing through small, old towns, nineteenth century Victorian houses, grand town halls, tree lined streets. It was a restful journey conducive to thought, meditation, contemplation. No crowds, arguments, excitement, meetings, conversations. No wonder, Tim thought, Jesus escaped to the mountain alone to pray!

As he pulled onto the tiny wooded road where his family cottage stood on a hill above a small lake, he felt a spiritual peace of a place settled by ministers in the early 1900s as a summer retreat. Peaceful. The autumn colors of the maple trees added brightness to the scene.

Tim trudged up the long narrow path to the small cabin—a hundred years of family artifacts and memories. The old lock on the door opened stiffly to reveal the inner room—old wood, high roof, fireplace. Just a small living room, two tiny bedrooms, a closet, a kitchen and a massive back porch facing the lake.

The quiet, peace, solitude. Tim, as usual at this rural retreat, slept fourteen hours the first night and awakened refreshed!

The next day he drove one and a half miles to the nearby small town–a fishing village on Lake Michigan now devoid of "summer people" just a few shops and small factory. The citizens lived mostly off the three summer months of "Lakies" and tourists. Most poor, humble people whose ancestors had settled in this remote North Woods during the timber days one hundred fifty years before. The "townies" immediately recognized a "lakie" but greeted Tim with polite, kind hospitality.

Rev. Tim always told his congregation that we are never "on vacation" from God and ministry–the Lord sends us opportunities everywhere to witness to Christ. On his first day of driving he entered a gas station store to hear a woman clerk telling her co-worker of a trying child custody battle in court when her husband had attacked her viciously. The woman said, "I could have said plenty about his drunkenness and cruelty, but I didn't." She then cried as she said "the judge recognized the lies and awarded custody to me."

Tim told her "You didn't return 'evil for evil' and God rewarded that!"

The clerk cried and said, "The moment you walked in the store I knew you were a minister!"

At the small grocery store in town, Tim got groceries, especially the fresh-caught fish in the area. Delicious.

Most days Tim meditated on Scripture and prayed, on the porch, before the fire in the cottage fireplace, on the small beach, and in walks through the woods. He often told friends "Four days up there is like a month's vacation!"

Sunday he attended the small church where he knew the minister and few member who took to lunch at a small cafe afterwards.

"How things in the town?" he asked him.

"Tim", Rev. Edward said, "we have the same problem as any city—drugs, crime, divorce, family abuse and break-ups. Kids confused about their identity. Suicide". But he went on to describe new Christian Family Center developed by local churches to provide counseling, charity and Biblical advice on Godly marriage and families—love, commitment, fidelity and the benefits of following the Lord's way. Tim visited the family facility housed in a big, old Victorian house, large wrap-around porch, twelve bedrooms, living, dining and rec rooms.

"Some homeless or abused live here in the center," the director told him. "We even have a kennel for the family pets, so residents can keep them!"

He continued, "Others have homes but come for counseling, help. We've seen God's Spirit move in so many family relationships that wanted reconciliation and healing."

"We could use this for our city," Tim said. "And every community."

After two weeks of rest and retreat, Tim felt ready to return home, refreshed and renewed.

As he drove homeward, he thought of all the Lord had done with WWJD and he thought "What will Jesus Do Now?!" Excitedly he called his wife when about to arrive home, looking forward to the continuing of this revival, renewal in Christ, morality, peace, decency, joy, love, responsibility, forgiveness, happiness, as God intended it. Fellowship, community, family, friendships, fulfillment.

As Tim pulled his car up in front of the church he saw a crowd gathered in front of two banners across the front of the church.

What Would Jesus Do NOW?
What WILL Jesus Do Now?

All his friends greeted him back: tough old Russ, healed Ted, wife Nancy, young son, Eric, youth leader Kevin; brother and sisters in Christ of all ages.

Then led by Loni, they broke into the song "What Would Jesus Do?" that she sang that first Sunday when he had had disasters and disappointments, launching the WWJD challenge.

The singing continued:

> *Oh Lord, please tell me*
> *What would Jesus do?*
> *With the addicted, the lonely and depressed*

To the lost and the hurt
Would He bend low to touch their heart?
Teach their soul which way to go.

Lord, please guide me and show me the way
To go about my everyday
Showing Your love and sharing Your name
Oh Lord, tell me, what would Jesus do

Oh Lord, please tell me
How I can make a difference
To help those you love and show them Your love
My Lord, show me by Your Word and Spirit
To do what Jesus would do

Give me the wisdom of Solomon
Give me the boldness of Esther
Guide me on the righteous path
Lord, give me the compassion as
Jesus gave to the woman at the well
O Lord, tell me what Jesus would do.

Then his wife came up to him, and placed a bracelet on his wrist with the initials WWJD-N for What Would Jesus Do NOW?!

Tim looked around and saw them all wearing such bracelets, reminding them of their commitment to Christ.

Study Guide

WWJD-NOW

Chapter 1
The Loss

Discussion Guide:

The cultural issues facing the church today are multi-layered and complex. WWJD-Now is a simple question that every follower of Christ should ask. Given the condition of the world around us, what would Jesus do about it?

How important is it to have a sense of sanctuary from the troubles and problems of the world?

What are the disciplines of a "well-ordered" soul? Are they really necessary given the immensity of need surrounding us?

Can the church building be a symbol of hope and healing for broken people?

Pastor Tim struggled with the need for internal order, with heartbreaking situations all around. Discuss.

Pastor Tim grew deeply burdened for people. Their problems were so immense he was overwhelmed. How would Jesus pray? What would he do?

Discuss the role of "prophet" and "priest" in the world? How important is it for the church to be "in the world"?

How important is it for the church to not be "of this world?"

Chapter 2
The Song

Discussion Guide:

Discuss what would Jesus do today with the lonely, depressed, and broken.

What are the depths of spiritual, social, and physical needs?

Who are the outcasts in our culture today?

How did Jesus respond to the culture around Him?

What are the barriers to getting involved in ministry to the broken segments in our cultures and families?

Personal Barriers?

Church Barriers?

Discuss how a church life can become dormant rather than dynamic and life-giving.

How can we use our gifts to answer the issues?

What discourages us?

What is the role of singing in revivals?

Chapter 3
The Question

Discussion Guide:

Discuss: John 10:27

What does it mean to hear Jesus' voice?

What does it mean to follow Jesus?

What are the implications of Jesus knowing His sheep?

What is the relationship between following Jesus and obedience?

What is your initial response to our anxiety, fears, and failures? What is a biblical response to these?

How would asking WWJD in my place affect my relationships with others?

Discuss the value of confession, repentance, and forgiveness and 1 John 1:9.

Discuss the role of the Holy Spirit as comforter, guide, and teacher in John 14 & John 16.

Chapter 4
The Meeting

Discussion Guide:

We do not know why Russ Turnbull responded that this WWJD stuff is ridiculous.

What could have been his emotional, intellectual, or spiritual barrier creating such a response?

What are the modern trends of church outreach? How effective have they been in making disciples?

Read 1 Corinthians 12 aloud.

How does God gift His body to minister as a kingdom of priests?

What is our mission as a kingdom of priests in 1 Peter 2:9?

Discuss the churches roles as a prophet of truth in the world and as a priestly advocate for a hurting world.

Chapter 5
Sunday Dinner

Discussion Guide:

What is the role of media, phones, and the internet in our lives?

What is the attraction and command of our attention from the phone? WWJD-N with the use of these devices?

How can we limit the influence of social media in our lives? How difficult will that be?

Discuss Romans 12:2 in its subtle influence in shaping, beliefs, motives, values, and attitudes.

Discuss Christ's Lordship and the spiritual stronghold that dominates our lives.

Chapter 6
WWJD-N

Discussion Guide:

Discuss Ralph Rosano turning down the big job offer. What would you have done with an attractive opportunity? WWJD-N?

Discuss the role of protecting and building the family and the priority of family over career.

If we seriously asked and applied WWJD-N, how would it affect us? In what ways would your life look different?

Why is easy to compartmentalize our work life from our spiritual life?

Discuss how the pursuit of the sensual "hedonistic" pleasure is a downward spiral of distraction.

Discuss Pastor Tim's roles as pastor to both Nick & Ralph.

How do we purposely live WWJD-N?

Read 1 Corinthians 13 aloud.

Discuss the relationship between love and truth, and the compassion of Christ.

Discuss the desire for fame and image for Loni's big break.

Chapter 7
Misery

Discussion Guide:

Following Christ is a walk in the light. We do not walk in darkness.

How should we deal with thoughts of revenge when wronged?

What are the conflicting emotions we struggle with when we are wronged?

Discuss the pleasure of sin being only for a season.

Chapter 8
The Temple

Discussion Guide:

Read 1 Corinthians 3:16 and discuss the implications of our body being the temple of God.

How does the culture view the human body?
    Self-expression
    Self-image

Someone once said we are living souls in a human body. Why did God create us?

What does the Bible teach concerning our use of words?

Read Ephesians 1 and discuss the blessings of a new identity in Christ.

How do your personal talents and gifts lead to a life of purpose?

Read Proverbs 31:10-31.

What are the virtues of biblical femininity?

What is the character of biblical manhood?

Discuss proper interactions between males and females.

Chapter 9
Blackmail

Discussion Guide:

What is the moral law within you and how does it work according to Galatians 5 in the law of reaping and sowing?

How does temptation work?

What draws a generation into sexual perversion?

What is a biblical view of human sexuality?

What did God intend in the purpose of marriage and children? What are the benefits of strong families?

What are the results of deviating from God's purpose in marriage?

Chapter 10
Revival

Discussion Guide:

In these noisy and distracting times, how important is peace, calm and quiet?

What does a biblical meditation look like Scripture, Music, Silence, Prayer, Listening, Hearing from God?

Discuss John 10:10 – The thief comes to kill, steal, and destroy, I have come that you might have life and life more abundantly.

Discuss the role of confession and repentance of sin 1 John 1:9.

How is the gospel, good news in a broken culture? He restores our souls, creates, loving committed relationships a sense of purpose, and amazing joy!

What role do worship and the Bible play in our dedication to Christ?

What is the role of the church service in fostering a sense of stability and security in life?

Discuss how Jesus brings freedom to power to overcome.

Chapter 11
Recovery

Discussion Guide:

WWJD with all the segments of brokenness in our society?

How does WWJD-Now address the crisis of broken families?

With the proliferation of addiction today WWJD?
    Adoption
    Individually
    In Counseling Centers
    In Halfway houses & community centers

Chapter 12
Attack

What is a proper response to opposition?

How can one discern a genuine move of God's spirit?

Discuss the role of prayer in God's work.

Chapter 13
Retreat

Discussion Guide:

Discuss the need for solitude.

How did Jesus retreat?

www.ingramcontent.com/pod-product-compliance
Lightning Source LLC
Chambersburg PA
CBHW070440010526
44118CB00014B/2123